Rainy Day Tea Time

by Edyta Sitar
for Laundry Basket Quilts

Landauer Publishing, LLC

Rainy Day Teatime

by Edyta Sitar

for Laundry Basket Quilts

Copyright © 2014 by Landauer Publishing, LLC

Rainy Day Teatime projects
Copyright © 2014 by Edyta Sitar for Laundry Basket Quilts

This book was designed, produced, and published by Landauer Publishing, LLC
3100 101st Street, Urbandale, IA 50322
www.landauerpub.com
515/287/2144   800/557/2144

President/Publisher: Jeramy Lanigan Landauer

Vice President of Sales and Administration: Kitty Jacobson

Editor: Jeri Simon

Art Director: Laurel Albright

Photographers
Project Photography: Edyta Sitar
Technique Photography: Sue Voegtlin

ISBN 13: 978-1-935726-67-8

This book printed on acid-free paper.

Printed in United States

10-9-8-7-6-5-4-3-2-1

FACEBOOK.COM/
LANDAUERPUBLISHING

YOUTUBE.COM/
LANDAUERPUBLISHING

PINTEREST.COM/
LANDAUERPUB

Table of Contents

Introduction 3

Supplies 3

Raw-Edge Appliqué 4

Binding 6

Apron 8

Book Cover 10

Hot Pad 11

Kitchen Curtains 12

Rainbow Napkin 13

Kitchen Towels 14

Place Mats 16

Tablecloth 18

Table Runner 19

Pillows 20

Painted Daisy Quilt 24

Market Tote 28

Appliqué Patterns 30

Introduction

Grab a cup of tea and discover your next rainy day project within the pages of this book. Most of the projects can be completed in an afternoon with a few basic sewing supplies. Dip into your stash to create pieces to complement your home.

Supplies

These are the fabrics and supplies I used for my projects. Feel free to use what you have on hand or use it as an excuse to visit your favorite quilt shop.

Fabrics
Edyta's Essentials batiks from Moda
Weave from Moda
Moda Toweling

Thread
Jellybean from Aurifil Thread
Edyta's Essentials from Aurifil Thread

Extras
Ric-Rac
Lace
Cotton Twill Tape
Light fusible webbing

While all the templates are provided for you in the book, you will be excited to know they are also available as dies from AccuQuilt®. Simple Shapes and Dancing Umbrella dies are new to the AccuQuilt® family and work with the GO!® fabric cutters. Needless to say, I am thrilled. As quilters, we love options for getting our projects done more quickly and this is certainly a great option. Visit accuquilt.com for more information.

Edyta

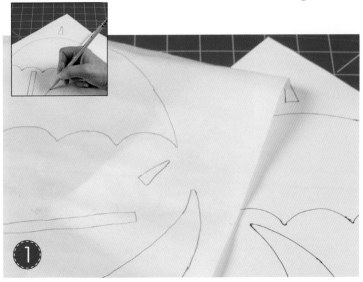

To prepare the appliqués, place the fusible webbing, paper side up, on the appliqué pattern. Using a pencil, trace the shapes onto the fusible webbing, leaving at least 1/4" between shapes. The shapes should also be at least 1/4" away from the edge of the webbing.

Trace all shapes needed for the project in the multitudes listed.

Note: All shapes in this book are reversed for this technique.

Cut out the appliqué shapes from the fusible webbing leaving at least 1/8" of fusible webbing around the outside of each shape. You may cut the fusible webbing from the center of the larger pieces if you wish.

Select the fabrics you wish to use with each shape.

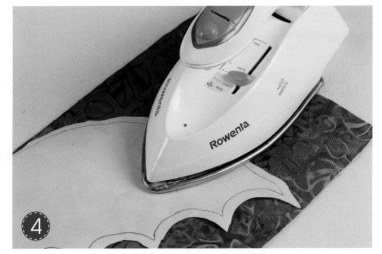

Place your fabric wrong side up and press to remove any wrinkles or creases.

Place your appliqué shapes, paper side up, on the wrong side of the fabric. Fuse each appliqué shape by gently pressing it with a dry iron following manufacturer's directions on fusible webbing.

Note: Do not over-press. I press for a few seconds and then let the fabric cool. If the shape is fused, I move to next step, if not I lightly press again.

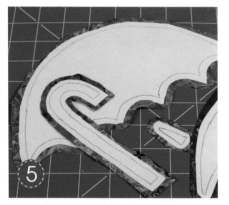

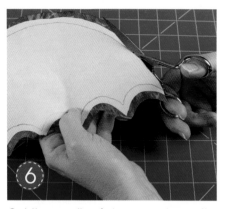

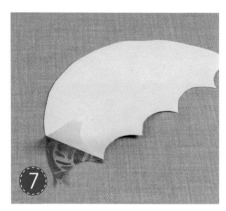

Trim excess fabric from around the shapes to prepare for final cutting.

Cut the appliqué shapes out exactly on the traced line. Achieve nice smooth edges by using the back blades of a sharp scissors and making long cuts.

Peel the fusible webbing paper from each shape.

Note: If you crease the edge of the paper it will peel off easier.

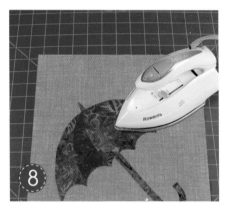

After all the paper is peeled off, place the shapes in the desired location on the background fabric.

Gently press the shapes with a dry iron to fuse in place.

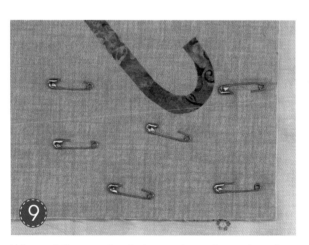

When all the appliqué shapes have been fused, layer the quilt top with the backing and batting.

Secure the three layers together with basting pins to prepare for stitching the appliqué shapes down.

Raw edge appliqué stitching is the quilting that holds the pieces in place. Make sure the pieces are fused securely in place before stitching.

Using the walking foot and a straight stitch, begin stitching 1/8" away from the edges of the appliqué shapes.

This stitch will hold all the shapes in place and create the raw edge appliqués. Always start stitching on the appliqué shape closest to the center of the quilt. Work your way out to the edges of the quilt until all the shapes have been stitched.

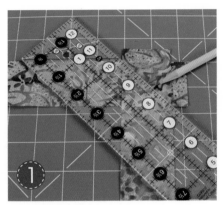

Cut 1-3⁄4" strips. The number of strips to cut will be determined by the project instructions. Lay one of the strips, right side up, on a flat surface. Place a second strip, wrong side up, on the first strip as shown. Draw a diagonal line from corner to corner on the top strip.

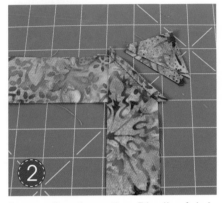

Sew on the drawn line. Trim the fabric 1/4" away from the sewn line.

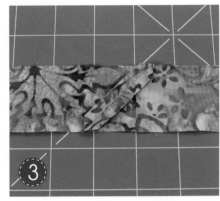

Press the seam allowances open. Continue until all the strips have been joined into one long continuous binding strip. Trim the "bunny ears".

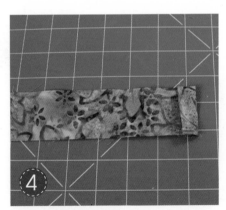

Fold one end of the binding strip over 1/2" and press.

Note: There are alternate methods to binding a quilt. This is how my grandmother taught me to do it. I love the clean look and ease of binding this way. This is a perfect method for lighter weight binding and especially smaller projects.

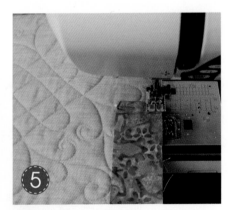

Align the raw edge of the binding strip with the raw edge of the quilted quilt top, batting and backing, right sides together. Begin sewing at the folded end of the binding strip. I generally begin my binding near the center point of the quilt top side edge.

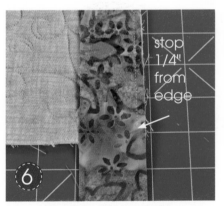

stop 1/4" from edge

Use a 1/4" seam allowance and sew the binding strip to the quilted quilt top, batting and backing. Stop 1/4" from the next edge of the quilted quilt top, batting and backing and backstitch.

Here's a Tip

I like to fold and lightly crease my binding at the 1/4" stopping point.

You may also mark the stopping point with a pin.

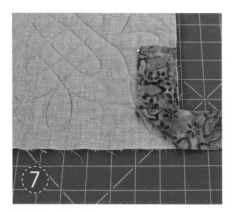

Fold the binding strip to create a 45-degree angle.

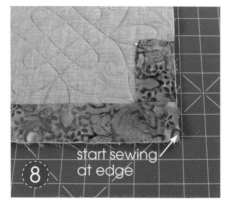

start sewing at edge

Fold the binding strip back over and align with the raw edge of the quilted quilt top, batting and backing. Start sewing at the edge with a 1/4" seam allowance. Continue sewing the binding strip to the quilt top, mitering each corner.

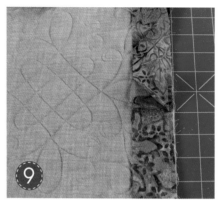

When you have reached the beginning point of the binding strip, cut the ending strip leaving 1/2" overlap. Sew a few stitches over the starting stitches.

Fold the binding strip to the stitched seam line. Iron or finger press the folded strip around the entire quilt top to create a crease.

Flip the quilt over so the backing is facing up. Turn the binding to the quilt back. Using a slipstitch sew it in place and fold the corners as you come to them. If you wish, use pins or binding clips to hold the binding in place as you stitch.

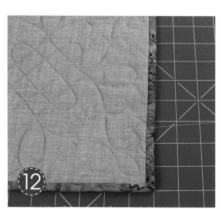

The result will be a flat, less bulky binding that still provides a double layer of protection for the edge of your beautiful quilt projects.

Apron

Everyone loves an apron and this one is so easy to make. For an extra twist, cut several aprons from a variety of fabric and shuffle the pieces. Switch the pockets and ties for several colorful creations. It's a perfect last-minute gift.

Materials

7/8 yard fabric for apron

Assorted fabric scraps for appliqué

Cutting

Note: Refer to the apron cutting layout for minimal fabric waste.

From the apron fabric, cut:

(1) 34" x 20" A rectangle for the apron skirt

(2) 40" x 3-1/2" B rectangles for the apron ties

(2) 8" x 9" C rectangles for the apron pockets

Note: I chose to only use 1 pocket on the featured apron.

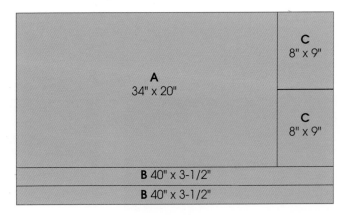

Assembling the Apron

1. Fold 1/4" to the wrong side of the bottom edge of apron skirt and press. Fold over again 1" and press. Stitch in place to complete the bottom hem of the apron skirt.

2. Fold the sides of the apron skirt 1/2" to the wrong side and press. Fold in half again and press. Stitch in place.

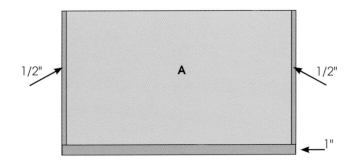

3. Fold 1/4" to the wrong side of the top of the pocket and press. Fold over again 1" and press. Top stitch the pocket hem. Fold the remaining three sides of the pocket 1/4" to the wrong side and press.

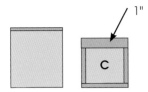

4. Place the pocket right side up on the apron skirt approximately 3" from the top and 6" from the side. Pin in place.

Note: Place the pocket on the side of the apron you prefer or place a pocket on both sides.

5. Beginning with a backstitch on the pocket edge, sew the pocket in place 1/8" from the edges.

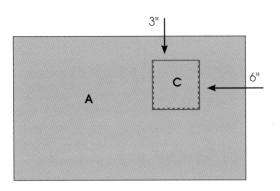

6. Sew the 40" x 3-1/2" strips together end to end to create a 79-1/2" x 3-1/2" continuous strip for the apron tie. Fold the strip in half widthwise, wrong sides together. Press.

7. Using a 1/4" seam allowance, stitch along the length of the strip leaving an opening of approximately 23". This opening will allow you to set in the apron skirt. Stitch the ends of the strip on a diagonal.

8. Turn the apron tie right side out and press.

9. Using a gathering stitch, gather the top of the apron skirt to approximately 23".

10. Position the center of the apron tie in the center of the apron skirt. Pin in place making sure the right side of the ties and right side of the apron skirt are facing. Sew the pieces. Hem the backside of the tie to the back of the apron skirt to hide the seam allowance. Press.

11. Top stitch around the apron tie and remove the gathering stitches from the apron skirt. Press.

Adding the Appliqué

1. Trace the appliqué patterns on page 30. Prepare the appliqué pieces referring to pages 4-5.

2. From the assorted fabric scraps, cut:
   (2) pattern A (stem; cut to desired length)
   (3) pattern D (leaf)
   (4) pattern E (leaf)
   (1) pattern K (bird top)
   (1) pattern L (bird bottom)

3. Position the appliqué pieces on the apron, referring to the photo on page 8 as a guide. Appliqué the shapes in place using your favorite method. Raw-edge appliqué was used along the edges of each of the appliqué pieces.

Book Cover

Protect your secret family recipes, treasured cookbook or journal in this elegant quick-to-stitch book cover.

Materials

1/3 yard gray fabric for book cover and inside pockets

Fat quarter lining fabric

1/8 yard binding fabric

Assorted fabric scraps for appliqué

12" x 18" batting

Cutting

From gray fabric, cut:
    (1) 10-1/2" x 16-1/2" rectangle for book cover front
    (2) 8" x 10-1/2" rectangles for inside pockets

From lining fabric, cut: (1) 12" x 18" rectangle

From binding fabric, cut: (1) 1-3/4" x wof binding strip

Assembling the Book Cover

1. Layer 10-1/2" x 16-1/2" book cover front rectangle, batting and 12" x 18" lining rectangle.

2. Quilt as desired. The book cover was quilted in a whimsical design. Trim the batting and lining even with edges of the book cover front.

Adding the Appliqué

1. Trace the appliqué patterns on page 30. Prepare the appliqué pieces referring to pages 4-5.

From the assorted fabric scraps, cut:
    (1) pattern A (stem; cut to desired length)
    (3) pattern D (leaf)
    (2) pattern E (leaf)
    (1) pattern K (bird top)
    (1) pattern L (bird bottom)

2. Position the appliqué pieces on the book cover front, referring to the photo as a guide. Appliqué the shapes in place using your favorite method. Raw-edge appliqué was used along the edges of each of the appliqué pieces.

Completing the Book Cover

1. With wrong sides together, fold each 8" x 10-1/2" inside pocket rectangle in half to measure 4" x 10-1/2". Press.

2. On the lining side of the cover, position an inside pocket at one short edge of the cover with pressed edge toward the center of the cover. Baste pocket in place along top, side and bottom edges of cover. Repeat for second pocket at the remaining short edge of cover.

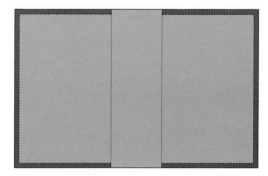

3. Referring to pages 6-7, bind all edges of the cover with the binding strip.

Hot Pad

Materials

10-1/2" fabric square for hot pad top

12" square batting

12" fabric square for hot pad backing

(1) 1-3/4" x 42" binding strip

Assorted fabric scraps for appliqué

Assembling the Hot Pad

1. Layer the hot pad top, batting and backing.

2. Quilt as desired. This hot pad was quilted with a large stippling design. Trim the batting and backing even with the edges of the hot pad top.

3. Bind the hot pad with the binding strip.

Adding the Appliqué

1. Trace the appliqué patterns on page 31. Prepare the appliqué pieces referring to pages 4-5.

   From the assorted fabric scraps, cut:
   - (1) pattern M (umbrella tip)
   - (1) pattern N (umbrella)
   - (1) pattern O (umbrella panel)
   - (1) pattern P (umbrella handle)

2. Position the appliqué pieces on the hot pad top, referring to the photo and diagram as a guide. Appliqué the shapes in place using your favorite method. Raw-edge appliqué was used along the edges of each of the appliqué pieces.

3. Referring to pages 6-7, bind all edges of the hot pad with the binding strip.

Kitchen Curtains

Bright appliqué and a strip of lace add a special touch to these kitchen curtains. These are the perfect quick and easy project for a rainy afternoon.

Materials

1-7/8 yards fabric for curtains

40"-long strip of your favorite lace
Note: The lace I used was 3-1/4"-wide.

Approximately 2 yards 1/2" twill tape

Assorted fabric scraps for appliqué

Cutting

From curtain fabric, cut:
- (1) 16" x 40" rectangle for top valance
- (2) 18" x 40" rectangles for bottom panels
- (2) 6" x 40" rectangles for bottom panels

From twill tape, cut:
- (18) 4"-long pieces

Assembling the Valance

1. Fold the 16" edges of the top valance 1/4" to the wrong side. Press. Fold 1/4" again and stitch in place. Press.

2. Fold the bottom edge of the top valance 1/4" to the wrong side. Press. Fold 1" again to create a bottom hem. Stitch in place.

3. Fold the top edge of the top valance 1/4" to the wrong side. Press. Fold 1-3/4" again and stitch in place. Press.

4. Top stitch a 1/4" away from the fold. Remember to leave an opening on the left and right sides to create a rod pocket for hanging. Press.

Assembling the Bottom Panels

1. Fold (9) 4" twill tape strips in half to form loops.

2. Beginning 1" from the edge, pin the loops in place on the right side of a 6" x 40" rectangle. Place the loops approximately 5" apart.

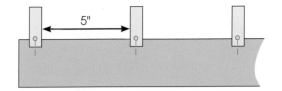

3. Fold the rectangle from step 2 in half, right sides together.

4. Sew the long raw edges of the rectangle together catching the ends of the loops in the seam. When you are finished sewing, you should have a fabric tube. Turn the tube right side out.

5. Roll the side edges of the tube in 1/2" when pressing. This is the top piece of the bottom panel. Make 2 and set aside.

6. Fold an 18" x 40" rectangle 1/4" to the wrong side on the top and sides. Press. Fold 1/4" again and press.

7. Fold the bottom edge 1/4" to the wrong side. Press. Fold 1" again to create a bottom hem. Stitch in place. Press. Repeat with the remaining 18" x 40" rectangle.

8. To connect the bottom panel pieces, pin the lace in place as shown. Top stitch the lace in place. Press. Make 2.

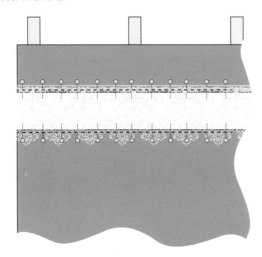

Adding the Appliqué

1. Trace the appliqué patterns on page 30. Prepare the appliqué pieces referring to pages 4-5.

From the assorted fabric scraps, cut:
    (4) pattern A (stem; cut to desired length)
    (4) pattern D (leaf)
    (10) pattern E (leaf)

2. Position the appliqué pieces on the bottom curtain panels. Remember, you will have a left and right bottom panel, so place the appliqués with this in mind. Refer to the photo on page 12 as a guide. Appliqué the shapes in place using your favorite method. Raw-edge appliqué was used along the edges of each of the appliqué pieces.

Rainbow Napkin

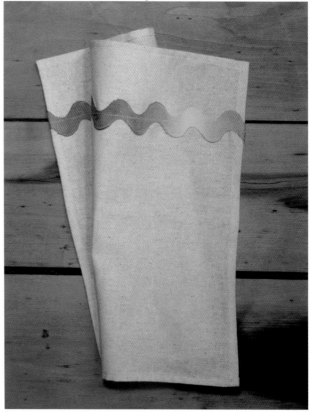

Materials

Makes one napkin

13" x 17" fabric rectangle for napkin

17" strip ric rac
Note: I used 3/4"-wide ric rac.

Assembling the Napkin

1. Lay the ric rac, right side up, approximately 3" from the bottom edge of the napkin. Pin in place.

2. Top stitch the ric rac in place using a matching or neutral thread.

3. Fold the top and bottom edges of the napkin 1/4" to the wrong side. Press. Fold 1/4" again and press. Repeat on the side edges. Make sure the edge of the ric rac rolls with the edge of the napkin.

4. Stitch around the entire napkin.

Kitchen Towels

Set aside a few hours to stitch up these simple kitchen towels. I used Moda Toweling fabric, which is already finished on two edges, to make the sewing process even speedier. This is also a great beginner project for a first-time appliquér.

Materials

Makes one towel

(1) 16" x 23" rectangle Moda Toweling fabric

(1) 6" strip 1/2" twill tape for loop

Assorted fabric scraps for appliqué

Assembling the Towel

1. Fold the 6" twill tape strip in half to make a loop.

2. Fold the 16" edges of the towel rectangle 1/2" to the wrong side. Press. Fold 1/2" again and press.

3. Slip the loop under the folded side edge of the towel, approximately 2" from a top corner. Pin the loop in place.

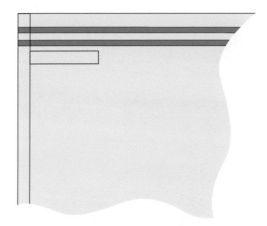

4. Top stitch the folded side edges. Remember to backstitch at the corners of the towel.

Adding the Appliqué

1. Trace the appliqué patterns on page 30. Prepare the appliqué pieces referring to pages 4-5.

    From the assorted fabric scraps, cut:
    (1) pattern A (stem; cut to desired length)
    (2) pattern D (leaf)
    (3) pattern E (leaf)

2. Position the appliqué pieces on the towel, referring to the photo as a guide. Appliqué the shapes in place using your favorite method. Raw-edge appliqué was used along the edges of each of the appliqué pieces.

Grannies Attic

Thank you to Grannies Attic for allowing me to spend the day exploring and photographing the projects in the book.

136 W. Michigan Avenue, Marshall, MI

Place Mats

Cutting

From Fabric A, cut: (4) 14" A squares

From Fabric B, cut: (4) 4-1/2" x 14" B rectangles

From backing fabric, cut: (4) 16" x 20" pieces

From binding fabric, cut:
(8) 1-3/4" x wof binding strips

Note: You will need 2 binding strips per place mat.

Assembling the Place Mats

1. Sew a 14" A square and 4-1/2" x 14" B rectangle right sides together as shown. Press the seam allowance toward the B rectangle to make the place mat top.

2. Layer the place mat top, batting and 16" x 20" backing piece together.

3. Quilt as desired. The place mats shown were quilted with a large all over stippling on Fabric A.

4. Trim the batting and backing even with the edges of the place mat top.

5. Join 2 binding strips into one continuous strip. Referring to pages 6-7, bind the place mat edges.

6. Repeat the steps to make the remaining 3 place mats.

Adding the Appliqué

1 Trace the appliqué patterns on page 30. Prepare the appliqué pieces referring to pages 4-5.

From the assorted fabric scraps, cut:
(4) pattern A (stem; cut to desired length)
(20) pattern E (leaf)

2. Position the appliqué pieces on Fabric B on the place mat top, referring to the photo as a guide. Appliqué the shapes in place using your favorite method. Raw-edge appliqué was used along the edges of each of the appliqué pieces.

Materials

Makes 4 place mats

7/8 yard Fabric A for place mat tops

1/2 yard Fabric B for place mat tops

1 yard backing fabric

(4) 16" x 20" pieces batting

1/2 yard binding fabric

Assorted fabric scraps for appliqué

Tablecloth

Materials

1-1/8 yards fabric for tablecloth

Assorted fabric scraps for appliqué

Cutting

From tablecloth fabric, cut:
   (1) 40" square

Assembling the Tablecloth

1. Fold all edges of the tablecloth 1/4" to the wrong side. Press. Fold 1" again and press.

2. Using a matching or neutral thread, top stitch all the edges in place.

Adding the Appliqué

1. Trace the appliqué patterns on page 30. Prepare the appliqué pieces referring to pages 4-5.

From the assorted fabric scraps, cut:
   (4) pattern A (stem; cut to desired length)
   (16) pattern D (leaf)
   (4) pattern E (leaf)

2. Position the appliqué pieces on the four corners of the tablecloth, using the photo as a guide. Appliqué the shapes in place using your favorite method. Raw-edge appliqué was used along the edges of each of the appliqué pieces.

Table Runner

Materials

1/2 yard fabric for table runner top

1/2 yard backing fabric

18" x 42" batting

1/4 yard binding fabric

Assorted fabric scraps for appliqué

Cutting

From table runner top fabric, cut:
    (1) 16" x 40" rectangle

From backing fabric, cut:
    (1) 18" x 42" rectangle

From binding fabric, cut:
    (3) 1-3/4" x wof binding strips

Assembling the Table Runner

1. Layer the 16" x 40" table runner top, batting and 18" x 42" backing rectangle.

2. Quilt as desired. The table runner was quilted in a whimsical design.

3. Trim the batting and backing even with the edges of the table runner top.

4. Join the binding strips into one continuous strip. Referring to pages 6-7, bind the table runner edges.

Adding the Appliqué

1. Trace the appliqué patterns on page 30. Prepare the appliqué pieces referring to pages 4-5.

From the assorted fabric scraps, cut:
    (4) pattern A (stem; cut to desired length)
    (6) pattern D (leaf)
    (12) pattern E (leaf)
    (2) pattern K (bird top)
    (2) pattern L (bird bottom)

2. Position the appliqué pieces on opposite ends of the table runner top, referring to the photo as a guide. Appliqué the shapes in place using your favorite method. Raw-edge appliqué was used along the edges of each of the appliqué pieces.

Pillows

Pillows add personality to any room. I have given you instructions for three pillows—one pieced and two appliquéd. Choose to make one or, better yet, make all three.

Materials for one appliquéd pillow

(1) fat quarter for pillow top

(1) 20" fabric square for pillow top backing

(1) 20" square batting

1/3 yard fabric for pillow back

1/8 yard binding fabric

Assorted fabric scraps for appliqué

Cutting

From pillow top fat quarter, cut:
    (1) 17-1/2" square

From pillow back fabric, cut:
    (2) 12" x 17-1/2" rectangles

From binding fabric, cut:
    (2) 1-3/4" binding strips

Assembling the Appliqué Pillow Top

1. Layer the pillow top, batting and pillow top backing.

2. Quilt as desired.

Adding the Appliqué

1. Choose the pillow you wish to make and trace the required appliqué patterns on pages 30-31. Prepare the appliqué pieces referring to pages 4-5.

Pillow A

From the assorted fabric scraps, cut:
    (2) pattern A (stem; cut to desired length)
    (4) pattern D (leaf)
    (4) pattern E (leaf)
    (2) pattern H (circle)
    (2) pattern I (circle)
    (2) pattern J (circle)

Pillow B

From the assorted fabric scraps, cut:
    (1) pattern K (bird top)
    (1) pattern L (bird bottom)
    (1) pattern M (umbrella tip)
    (1) pattern N (umbrella)
    (1) pattern O (umbrella panel)
    (1) pattern P (umbrella handle)

2. Position the appliqué pieces on the pillow top, referring to the photo on page 20 as a guide. Appliqué the shapes in place using your favorite method. Raw-edge appliqué was used along the edges of each of the appliqué pieces.

Finishing the Pillow

1. Square the pillow top to 17-1/2", trimming any excess batting and backing.

2. Fold 1" to the wrong side along a 17-1/2" edge of both pillow back rectangles. Press. Fold 1" again and top stitch in place. Press.

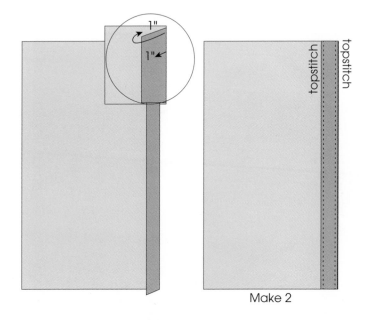

Make 2

3. Layer the pillow backs on the quilted pillow top, wrong sides together. The pillow backs will overlap. Baste around the edges to hold the pieces together.

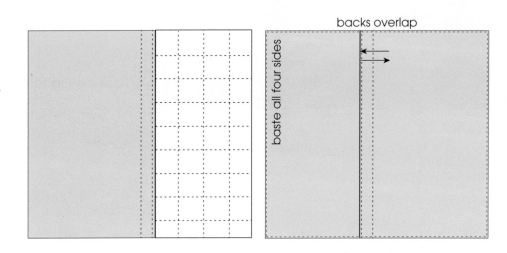

4. Join the binding strips into one continuous strip. Referring to pages 6-7, bind the pillow edges.

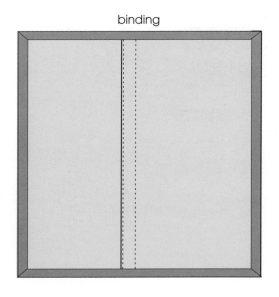

Materials for pieced pillow

1/4 yard background fabric

(1) 20" fabric square for pillow top backing

(1) 20" square batting

1/3 yard fabric for pillow back

1/8 yard binding fabric

Assorted light and dark fabric strips
*Note: I used a variety of fabric scraps left over from
other projects.*

Cutting

From background fabric, cut:
    (3) 4" x 17-1/2" rectangles

From pillow back fabric, cut:
    (2) 12" x 17-1/2" rectangles

From binding fabric, cut:
    (2) 1-3/4" binding strips

Assembling the Pieced Pillow

1. Sew the assorted light and dark fabric strips together, alternating the light and dark, to make a panel. From the panel, cut (2) 4" x 17-1/2" scrappy rectangles.

2. Lay out the 3 background rectangles and 2 scrappy rectangles, alternating them as shown in the photograph on page 20. Sew the pieces together to create the pillow top.

3. Layer the pillow top, batting and pillow top backing.

4. Quilt in the ditch on the scrappy rectangles and quilt vertical lines over the background rectangles.

5. Square the pillow top to 17-1/2", trimming any excess batting and backing.

6. Fold 1" to the wrong side along a 17-1/2" edge of both pillow back rectangles. Press. Fold 1" again and top stitch in place. Press.

7. Layer the pillow backs on the quilted pillow top, wrong sides together. The pillow backs will overlap. Baste around the edges to hold the pieces together.

8. Join the binding strips into one continuous strip. Referring to pages 6-7, bind the pillow edges.

Painted Daisy Quilt

Finished Block Size: 12" x 12"
Finished Quilt Size: 48" x 48"

Materials

7/8 yard total assorted multi-color batik fabrics for blades

2-1/4 yards gray fabric for blades, background and borders

5/8 yard taupe fabric for background

2-1/2" x 23" medium gray strip for center circles

3/8 yard binding fabric

3 yards backing fabric

52" x 52" batting

Fusible webbing for center circles

Cutting

From assorted multi-color batik fabrics, cut:
    (144) 1-1/2" x 4-1/2" strips for blades

Note: You can cut (26) 1-1/2" strips per 4-1/2" x wof strip

From gray fabric, cut:
    (6) 4-1/2" x wof strips. From the strips, cut:
        (144) 1-1/2" x 4-1/2" strips for blades.

(3) 6-1/2" x wof strips. From the strips, cut:
    (18) background pieces using the template on page 27.

(4) 6-1/4" x wof border strips.

From taupe fabric, cut:
    (3) 6-1/2" x wof strips. From the strips, cut:
        (18) background pieces using the template on page 27.

From binding fabric, cut:
    (5) 1-3/4" x wof binding strips.

Assembling the Blocks

1. Sew a 1-1/2" x 4-1/2" multi-color batik strip and 1-1/2" x 4-1/2" gray strip right sides together to make a strip set. Press. Make 144 strip sets.

2. Cut a blade from each strip set using the template on page 27.

3. Sew 4 blades together to create a block quarter, pressing the seams in the same direction. Make 36 block quarters.

Note: Chain piecing will speed the sewing process along.

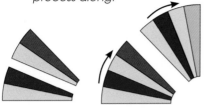

Make 36

4. Separate the block quarters into sets of 4. You should have 9 sets.

5. Referring to the diagram, sew gray background pieces to 2 block quarters in each set. Sew taupe background pieces to the remaining block quarters. Press the seam allowances toward the background pieces.

Note: Before sewing, mark the center of each background piece and match it to the block quarter's center seam. I position my block quarter on the bottom and background piece on top when sewing. I also like to make my stitch slightly smaller, which allows me to stitch around the curve more easily.

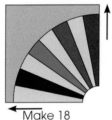

Make 18   Make 18

6. Sew 4 of the sets made in step 5 together to make a block. Alternate the gray and taupe background pieces around the block. Refer to the diagram below for pressing directions. Make 9 blocks.

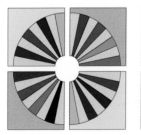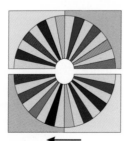

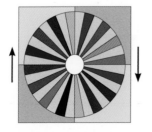

7. Trace 9 center circles onto the fusible webbing using the template on page 27. Cut out the center of the shapes leaving approximately a 1/4" of a circle of fusible webbing. Iron to the medium gray fabric strip. Cut the circles from the fabric strip. Fuse a medium gray circle in the center of each block making sure the fusible webbing is adhered to the block fabric.

Cut out

8. Appliqué the center circles to the blocks. Turn the blocks over and press from the back. Make 9 blocks.

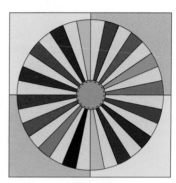

Make 9

Assembling the Quilt Top

1. Referring to the Quilt Diagram, lay out the blocks in 3 rows with 3 blocks in each row. Check to make sure you have positioned the taupe background piece in the top left corner of each block.

2. Sew the blocks together in rows. Press seams in one direction, alternating direction from row to row.

3. Sew the rows together. Press.

Quilt Diagram

Adding the Borders

1. Sew a border strip to the quilt top beginning at the bottom right corner of the quilt top. Stop sewing approximately two-thirds from the left bottom corner. Press the partially sewn seam toward the border.

2. Sew the remaining border strips to the quilt top in the following order: right side border, top border, left side border. Press seams toward border strips. Finish sewing the bottom border.

Finishing the Quilt

1. Layer the quilt top, batting and backing.

2. Quilt as desired.

3. Join the binding strips into one continuous strip. Referring to pages 6-7, bind the quilt edges.

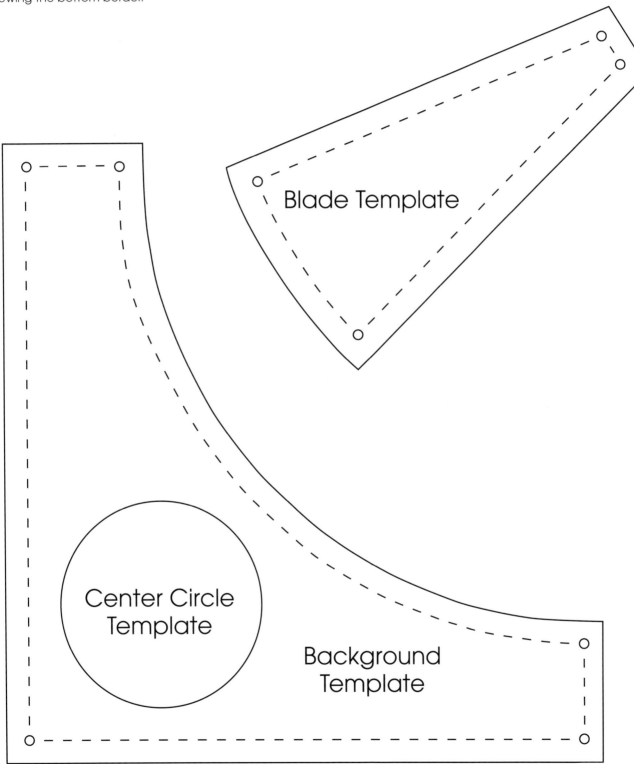

Blade Template

Center Circle Template

Background Template

Market Tote

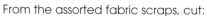

Materials

1/2 yard fabric for tote body

7/8 yard 1"-wide twill tape for handles

1/8 yard accent fabric for tote top

Assorted fabric scraps for appliqué

Cutting

From tote body fabric, cut:
 (1) 34" x 16" A rectangle

From 1"-wide twill tape, cut:
 (2) 1" x 16" strips for handles

From accent fabric, cut:
 (2) 3-1/2" x 16" C rectangles

Assembly

1. Fold the fabric A rectangle in half widthwise, wrong sides together, and lightly crease to identify the front and back of the tote. Position a handle on the 16" side of the fabric A rectangle, wrong side up. Each handle end should be approximately 4" from the edge. Place a C rectangle, wrong side up, on the fabric A rectangle aligning raw edges and covering handle ends. Stitch the pieces together, catching the handle ends in the seam allowance. Repeat with remaining handle on the opposite side of the A rectangle.

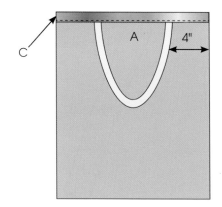

2. Flip the C rectangles to the right side of the fabric A rectangle. Fold the raw edges under 1/4" and top stitch the edges. Press.

Adding the Appliqué

1. Trace the appliqué patterns on page 31. Prepare the appliqué pieces referring to pages 4-5.

From the assorted fabric scraps, cut:
 (1) pattern M (umbrella tip)
 (1) pattern N (umbrella)
 (1) pattern O (umbrella panel)
 (1) pattern P (umbrella handle)

2. Position the appliqué pieces on the right side of the fabric A rectangle, referring to the photo on page 28 as a guide. Appliqué the shapes in place using your favorite method. Raw edge appliqué was used along the edges of each of the appliqué pieces.

Finishing the Tote

1. Fold the fabric A rectangle in half widthwise, wrong sides together. Sew the sides of the rectangle together using a scant 1/4" seam allowance.

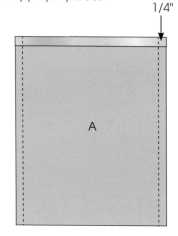

2. Turn the bag inside out, so right sides are facing. Sew the sides together using a 1/4" seam allowance. This will protect the seams from fraying.

3. To box the bottom of the tote, create a small triangle on each bottom corner. Measure 1-1/2" from the point and stitch as shown.

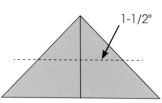

Simple Shapes
Appliqué Patterns

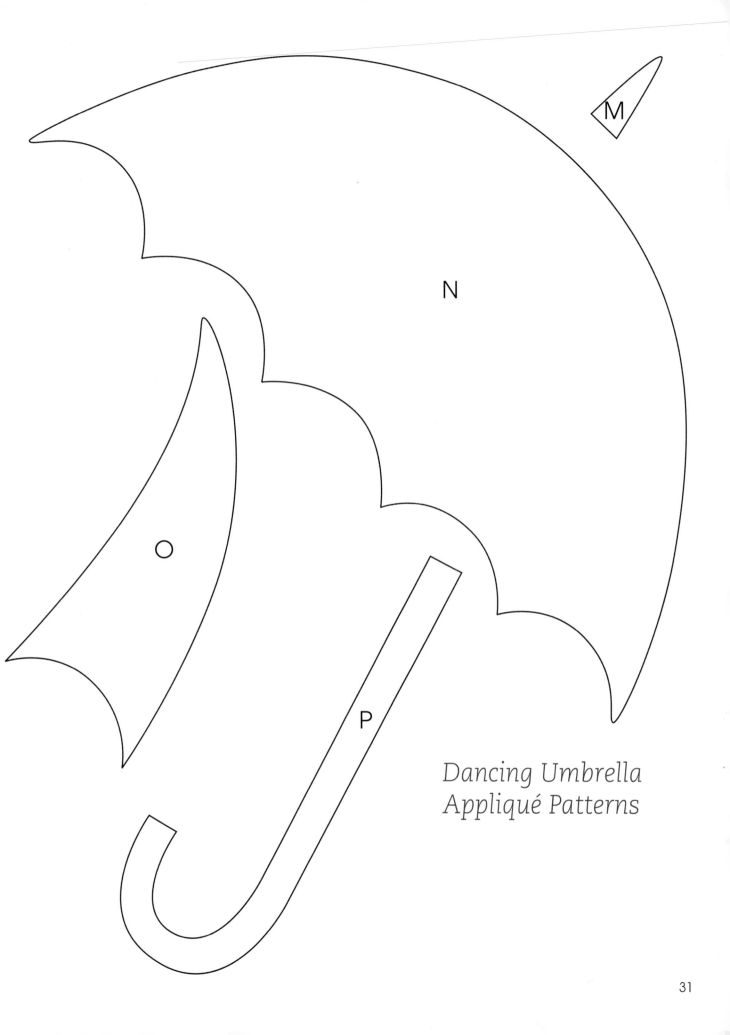

M

N

O

P

Dancing Umbrella
Appliqué Patterns

Edyta Sitar is proud to carry on a family tradition that fabrics and threads have seamlessly stitched together through the generations.

Her true love for quilting and her quilter's spirit shines through in her classes, workshops, and presentations. She travels all over sharing her passion, connecting to and inspiring quilters of all levels by sharing personal and stimulating stories about the quilts she makes.

Quilting has opened a door to another world for Edyta, one in which she can express herself, create beautiful designs, and release her artistic passion. The combination of inspiration from nature, a love for fabric, a keen eye for color, and her family teachings blended into the recipe for developing a flourishing talent for designing quilts, fabrics, and quilting patterns.

"My children and my husband are my greatest motivation, providing the basis that you can accomplish anything you want if you just set your mind to it. Being able to do what I love and share this love with others is the greatest feeling and reward I could imagine! This is the Cinderella dream for me."

As the owner and co-founder of Laundry Basket Quilts, her work has been published in magazines world-wide and her quilts have received numerous awards.

Edyta resides in Marshall, Michigan, with her husband and children where she enjoys creating beautiful patterns for Laundry Basket Quilts and designing splendid fabrics for MODA.